WHAT ARE P[eople Saying About]

Manhood on the Line?

As a man, a life coach, a relationship coach and minister, I connected with this book on multiple levels. I felt like I was in a barbershop or on a street corner having a conversation with Don. His authenticity, humor, transparency and honesty kept me engaged in his story. I laughed out loud several times!!

Brother Don was raw, real and very transparent with his "manhood"; which will undoubtedly give other men permission to do the same. The reflective questions at the end of each chapter will force men to do more than read this book, they'll have to think!!

We need this! Thank you, Don, for sharing your story.

—Rodney Gray, Minister, Life - Leadership - Relationship Coach
Freedom Success Solutions LLC

Manhood on the Line is at times funny, shocking and raw. The transparency that Don writes with will prove to be inspiring for many, while gut wrenching and thought provoking for others. Every man will see himself somewhere in this book. If you are a man looking to grow and evolve as a person, this book is for you. If you are someone who works with men or if you are a woman looking to gain insight into the male perspective, *Manhood on the Line* is a must read! Well done!

—William Batts, LMSW

THIS BOOK IS PHENOMENAL! It's not every day that you hear this level of transparency and vulnerability from a man when it comes to the topic of love as it was shared in this book. As much as there is a need for stronger, black men in our community, the need is much greater in our families. Don is creating a shift in how we as women understand and relate to our men...he's starting the process of healing between us.

He challenges men to evaluate their past and how it's surfacing in their present, to look themselves in the mirror and discover all the areas where they can be better to themselves, honest with themselves and the ones they love. But what I love most about this book is how his perspective of love evolved. Yes, love and feelings of being on Cloud-9 are great in the beginning, but to stand the test of time and create a solid foundation to grow on, truth and the ability to harmoniously adjust is key!

This is a MUST READ for everybody!!

—Dominique Clark
Best Selling Author – She's Valuable | Relationship Expert | Red Carpet Correspondent + Host | HER Mentor, DClark & Company

MANHOOD
ON THE
LINE

A REAL MAN OWNS HIS SH*T

DONALD F. BARNETT III
FOREWORD BY PAUL CARRICK BRUNSON

© 2018 by Donald Barnett III

Published by Tanya Barnett Enterprises, LLC.

White Plains, Maryland

Printed in the United States of America

ALL RIGHTS RESERVED. This book contains material protected under international and federal copyright laws and treaties. Any unauthorized reprint or use of this material is prohibited. No part of this book may be reproduced or transmitted in any form or by any means, electronic
or mechanical, including photocopying, recording, or by any information storage and retrieval systems without express written permission from the publisher except in the case of brief quotations embodied in critical articles and Reviews.

You will see my reference my wife as Ve or Vedia throughout the book. That is her given name that her father and I call her. Everyone else calls her by her middle name, Tanya.

Scripture taken from New King James Bible. Copyright © 1988

Back cover photograph – E.Y.E. Imagery

Book jacket design – Germancreative

ISBN 978-0997493757 (pbk.)

Library of Congress Control Number(LCN) 2018909427

Dedication

I dedicate this book to my father, the Late Donald F. Barnett Jr. and to my Grandmother, the late Ruth Barnett. They did their very best they could with what they had in order to give me a life better than the one they had. My father taught me what he knew about being an honest man and an attentive father. My grandmother gave me lots of love and good food. She taught me the most valuable skill I would ever use, how to pray.

To my Great Aunt, Geneva Barnett (Granny): thank you for picking up the torch and running with it after my grandmother and father were called home to be with the Lord. You prayed for me through their deaths and through my transition to being on my own. You chastised me when I strayed to the left and to the right but loved me just the same. For this, I am forever grateful.

To Batts: You are truly my brother from another mother. You have seen the very best and the very worst of me, yet, you never judged me. You have always been a source of wisdom and an on-the-spot prayer partner. You are a great uncle to my children and I thank God for you. I love you brother.

To Dion B.: I know your prayers and talks helped me and Ve navigate marriage. It's funny how you would call or just show up at our house out the blue just when we needed you the most. You never gave up on us and you prayed us through some rough patches. I will forever be grateful to you for loving me like a brother.

My Frat brothers: RQQ to the Bruhz, Bloody Beta Chapter - My line brothers, 8 Sons of Sacrifice, AKA 94 Phunk - Phene, Blair, Danny, Shawn, Ron, Leroy, and Carl. I love y'all! Long live the 94 PHUNK! Special thanks to these Bruhz: Mike B., Norm B, Nigel P., Quebec L., Thomas M., Chris S., Tony Z., Darryl H., Hervie B., Damaas S., Marlon C., Eric P., Jamie Y., Tracy B. and Lou R. Thank you for the uplift.

To my sister, Tiffany Barnett, my niece Dez, and my nephews Quinton and Quincy, I love you.

To my in-laws, Rodney and Ruth Walker: thank you for trusting me with and for giving me your baby girl's hand in marriage. Being married over forty years is a huge accomplishment. I hope Ve and I experience this and more. Pop, I especially thank you for showing how to navigate through being a husband and a great father. I love you.

To my three wonderful children, Jakim, Doni and Gabi: I love each of you in your own unique way. You've enhanced my life in ways I could never imagine. To watch you grow up to be the loving, giving and kind young adults you've become, is an honor. I am very proud to be your dad.

To my grandson, W. Malcolm Walker (Dink): You are another reason for me to live each and every day. I will teach you one of the most important things my grandmother taught me - how to pray.

To my lovely wife, Ve (aka my Girlfriend), thank you for pushing me to be a better version of me. Even though I took you through the ringer and back, you never waivered in your love for me. You've always supported my dreams, regardless of how far-fetched they were. I love you and I thank God for you being my wife.

Table of Contents

Foreword	13
Preface	19
1 What Did I Just Do?	29
2 You Said He's Just A Friend	61
3 If Only My Dad Had Been There	71
4 Dear Mama	79
5 I Don't Want To Go Home	91
6 Nah, I'm Good	105
7 Finally, Owning My Sh*t	117
8 Counseling - Who Needs That?	135
9 Don't Call It A Comeback	147
10 The Game Plan	157

MANHOOD
ON THE
LINE

*A REAL MAN OWNS HIS SH*T*

DONALD F. BARNETT III
FOREWORD BY PAUL CARRICK BRUNSON

Foreword

Brothers, very rarely do we come across a book from a man's perspective about his childhood, past hurts, and disappointments. Most books on those topics are written by women for women. Their authors seem to effortlessly share their traumatic stories and through their transparency, help women heal.

On the other hand, books for men that deal with these issues are mainly scholarly in nature. Then there are the self-help books that provide solid theory but many of the authors have little real-world practice to support their findings.

Manhood on the Line is like no other book before it. This book is full of one man's raw emotion. It deals with such issues as the impact of absentee parenting, infidelity, and more. All from a man's perspective. This book shares how these issues affected Brother Don's life and what he did to overcome and save his marriage in the process of saving himself.

Manhood on the Line is a tool to help you take your life in your own hands. Like some men, I'm sure you are asking, "Paul, what do you mean by that? I've got the house, the job, and the money I've dreamed about. I'm good." Or you may be saying, "Paul, I tried to live right but my father wasn't in my life. I was abused. I was in a gang. I did time behind bars. I've done so much wrong in my life, surely I can't change now."

I say to you, this is not true. Change always occurs when you truly want it.

Today, I challenge you to believe you can take your life in your own hands. You are not a victim of your circumstances. You never were. You may have been made to believe you are and because of this, you may have tried to work, to drink, and to maybe even sex the pain away. Only to wake up and feel that the pain didn't go anywhere. If anything, that pain is pressing on you, making it hard for you to breathe, to think, and love.

Don felt the same way and the beauty in his story is that he is no longer there. He had to face his past, own his mess, and do the self-work to become the victor. He is a beacon of hope for men just like you. He often says if he can overcome his life circumstance, so can the next brother.

Don hopes that being honest and sharing his ugly truth about what he experienced in his life will strengthen you. He had to work hard to overcome these challenges and is now sharing his victories, so you too will gain the courage to do the same.

When you do this, not only will your life improve, but so will the lives of those whom you love the most – your friends, your significant other, and your children. Once this transformation happens, your community then benefits from the new and improved you.

Don is an authentic and transparent brother who has experienced things most of us would never share, for fear of being judged by other men. I would even venture to say most of us would not share the things in our past we are most embarrassed about to the woman in our life either.

The time has come for all of us to take stock of where we are at this very moment. Are you living to your greatest potential or are you living stuck behind your past hurts, failures, and disappointments? Don wrote this book to be a tool to help you get honest with yourself.

Michael Jackson said, "We all need to look at the man in the mirror." When was the last time you did this? When was the last time you did an honest assessment of where you are? What did you see? Was there room for improvement?

As a man, I too have had to overcome failures and disappointments to be the husband, father, mentor, and teacher I've become. This was not an overnight process. I lost my best friend and it took the wind out of me. I made a choice to not wallow in his death, but to honor his memory in love and the things I do.

Have you ever experienced breathtaking pain?
Have you felt loss so bad that you had to fight to make it through yet another day?

You are not alone. Don has too.

This book is about hope. This book shows that you can overcome, and that success is in you, if you look hard enough. You must do the work, though. Don gives tips to begin the process of not only facing your fears, but also dealing with the pain of dropping the ball, making the wrong choices, and even saying and doing things you are ashamed of. Brother, it's your turn to begin the healing process.

As you read through the pages of this book, consider taking stock of your past and how it may be affecting you right now. Take time to recognize repetitive behaviors that are counterproductive to what you want in life and where you want to go.

Examine the way you talk to your girlfriend or wife, as well as your children. How would you feel if someone spoke to them the way you do? As men, we have a responsibility to set the tone for our families and communities. They need us. Other brothers need us.

I encourage you to give yourself grace if you don't have it all together. I dare say most men don't. Self-awareness is the first step to healing. Give yourself permission to be vulnerable and to heal as you read this book. Once you begin to heal, you can grow.

Allow Don's story of loss, lies and then true love, to inspire you to hold on another day. After all, you have nothing to lose yet everything to gain. Your future is bright. We are in this together.

Paul Carrick Brunson

Preface

I wrote this book to help men like you and me to become better men, husbands, and fathers. I want to encourage men like us to look in the mirror and to ask ourselves, "Am I living my life to my fullest potential? Am I a great son, friend, father, or husband? Am I a leader and positive role model in my community?"

I am asking you these questions because I had to ask myself these same questions. When life was tough, I can honestly tell you that I wasn't a good husband, father, or friend. I was simply existing. I had given up. Well, brother, I don't want that for you another day. Giving up is one of the easiest things to do in life. So, I challenge you to:

Stand up and take ownership of your actions:
- Forgive not just yourself but people who may have hurt you in the past.
- Stop living from a place in the past, full of anger, pain, unforgiveness, and resentment.

- Understand your past and your present can not share the same space if you want to move forward in your personal life and in your relationships.

My goal is to inspire men, just like you, to work through the challenges of not just being a man but also through your personal challenges. The truth is that we are not going to have all the answers for every situation we face in life.

I know, you've been told to "Man up," but I want you to know that in some instances, this is not possible. You may have moments when you feel weak and helpless. I got you! So did I. We will get through that, together.

I want to help you break free from the misconceptions of what being in a committed relationship or marriage will be. You know what I am talking about. Those lies that may have been passed down from your father, uncles, cousins, your homies, movies, and even your own past experiences. I want to help men like us own their truths, no matter how raw and ugly those truths are.

#RealTalk — I want you to face yourself in the mirror and tell yourself that you once and for all own your sh*t! This is the first step to growth. After this, you will be ready to put in the work to become a better man, husband, and even a better father.

When I made the decision to look at myself in the mirror, I was depressed by what I saw. However, I loved my wife and children so much that I chose to finally recognize and own my ugly truth — I was not a whole man. I struggled with issues that made me question if I should go home to my wife and kids or entertain the foolishness of other women.

Analyzing myself was the first step, the catalyst for change in my life. Seeing it right there and then, digging really deep to own my truth, gave me the courage to want to become a better husband and father. I also knew I needed help and with the persistence of my wife, I finally chose to go see a therapist.

In the African American community and amongst some men, counseling is a major taboo. Well, one of my goals is to crush this taboo that has so many of us suffering in silence. I will be sharing my counseling experience with you. It was, truly, the best decision I have ever made.

My initial thoughts never made it into this book because the writing process took on a life of its own. Instead of glossing over my issues with myself and with my wife, I was challenged by a good friend to be totally transparent in *Manhood on the Line*. That was scary and I almost lost my lunch when she suggested this to me.

I struggled with sharing my inner issues that had me constantly questioning my manhood in the sense of being true to my commitment to my family and to God. In my transparency and honesty, I knew my story would be a blessing to you.

I want you to laugh out loud and if need be, cry. It's okay. No one will take your manhood card. Take your time in reading this book. Read it twice, highlight, circle, or do whatever else you feel is necessary to get the meat of what I am sharing.

Ultimately, my hope is to leave you with powerful nuggets and realistic tips to ponder and to use for years to come. My desire is that this book will encourage you to want to become a better version of you, which will lead to you becoming a better man.

This book is all about you and how you can be empowered to implement positive change in your life – today! Man, imagine when you get free! Then you can help the brothas you talk to or kick it with.

Please take your time when going through this book. Seriously! I intentionally made sure the size was large enough to write in and not too long that you wouldn't finish it. I know how we do. We look at a book and immediately think, "Nah bruh, this joint is too long. I'm not reading that." I challenge you to think differently when opening this book. Your life depends on it.

I placed a section called the GAME PLAN in the back for you to write down your plans for change as well as personal reflections. I really want you to use this area as a tool to write out a plan for positive change in your life.

If things pop out at you while reading, write it down in this book and then let me know via social media; my contact information is @DonBarnetIII on IG and TW. I urge you to be proactive in being the agent of change for not only yourself, but for your family and your community.

Now, grab a pen and find a quiet place to read. If you retreat to your man cave with a beer or two so you can read this book in peace, at least put the game on mute. You can't watch the game and pay attention to this book at the same time. I know, I've tried it.

I am not ashamed to say that I survived years of being in a whirlwind of negative emotions and destructive choices that were equally toxic. I am happy that I am finally standing on solid ground in my life and in my marriage. I am thankful that I am now owning my sh*t. SO CAN YOU! After all, your manhood is on the line.

Prayer for My Brothers

God, I come before You to say thank you and to lift you up because You are mighty. With You all things are possible. I am a testimony to that. Touch the brother's heart and mind who is about to read this book. May his heart and mind be open to receiving the truth and the healing only You give.

Let the words written within the chapters of this book encourage him to take responsibility for his own life and relationships. Remove from him excuses and lies that are hindering him from being a caring and loving man.

When it comes to interactions with his fiancé/wife, may he be a loving man who is "swift to hear and slow to speak, slow to wrath." (James 1:19) May his heart be full of love, understanding and forgiveness for his wife. Give him the strength, the courage, and the tools he needs to be a better man, husband, and father.

In Jesus' Name Amen!!!!

Not everything that is faced can be changed; but nothing can be changed until it is faced.

-James Baldwin

1 What Did I Just Do?

A happy man marries the girl he loves, but a happier man loves the girl he marries.

African proverb

It was in March 1998 that I met Vedia. People would call it a coincidence: I had a doctor's appointment with a new doctor. It just so happened to be on the first day Ve started her new job. She was the medical technician in this doctor's office.

Just to set the record straight, at the end of that appointment, she gave me her cell phone number, the number to her apartment, and her parents' home number before I left the doctor's office that day.

I know, I know... a brother got mad game that blows the ladies away every time. Anyway, I was really digging her. While I was checking her out, I noticed she had pretty toes as she slipped her foot out of her slides. She also had a 'phat' booty. Pretty feet and a 'phat' booty are a must on my list of non-negotiables. Hey! What can I say? I'm a simple guy.

We only dated for about a month before she went totally crazy on me. I was being all nice to her, but she acted like I was getting on her nerves, like I was a chump.

Occasionally, I would go by her job to bring her either a $.99 rose from 7-11 (you know the one that has the plastic water cap on the bottom of it), a salad, Reese's Cups, or some other thing I learned that she liked to eat.

Can you believe this chick said I was smothering her? What woman in her right mind doesn't want a great guy to treat her with respect? I'm just saying, I wasn't trying to get in her drawls that early in the talking phase.

But since she wanted to act like I was a chump and like she didn't want any bother out of me, I bounced. She didn't have to tell a brother to get lost but one time. After all, I was living in the DC area – where all the fine honeys were, so I kept it moving.

We reconnected at the end of that year after having not talked to each other since April. We hung out a few times before we started talking again.

Then one night, while we were on the phone, Ve said what most women say when they don't want any pushback from a man. She blurted out that "the *LORD SAID"* I was going to be her husband! I hate when people use the Lord to get you not to challenge what they are saying. I wondered if she was doing the same thing.

Now, I'm sure you've also had a woman tell you the same thing. That stuff ain't cute. Actually, it's a turn-off. I wasn't going to fall for the Okie-Doke so soon after reconnecting with this chick. Plus, she had a kid and I told myself I would never marry a woman with a kid. I cracked up on the inside and thought, "Here we go...."

I didn't want to hurt her feelings, so I replied in my most chill way, "Oh yeah? Well, He ain't tell me nothing, so I will wait to hear from Him." You know when you let people know you waiting on the Lord too, they leave you alone.

Well guess what, brother? I took the bait. Nah, I'm joking. But seriously, I fell in love with this woman not long that conversation. I really knew deep down in my heart she was going to be my wife. I cannot remember what happened after I got that revelation. I just knew she was the one.

Soon after that, I took Ve and her daughter to Pennsylvania to get used to being around my Great Aunt "Granny" and the rest of the Barnett family. My Granny don't play none of that. If Ve passed the "Granny test," I would have a winner and she would be as good as gold.

My family instantly received Gabi and Ve into the family. Before I knew it, my family loved them, and my Granny asked if I thought she was the one. Of course, I played it off and told Granny that I wasn't thinking about that at all.

I also introduced her to my frat brothers. I told them about her and they dubbed her "the little nurse." She had to pass their litmus test too. Real Talk: if they weren't feeling her, I am not sure how this would have played out. Thankfully they thought she was cool, so I knew she must be alright.

A few weeks after that, I introduced her to my sister and my niece. Her daughter and Gabi were two years apart, so of course they hit it off. I was so excited about her naturally getting along with my people that I was eventually settled on the fact that I was marrying this woman.

We set a June 1999 wedding date. The events leading up to that were a blur. I was so excited that I was going to marry my queen. My family loved her, her family loved me. What else did we need? Cue in the scary music from *JAWS*.

Our wedding day was a day that I eagerly anticipated after realizing that this woman was going to be my future wife. It was a day that I looked forward to sharing with my family, my friends, and my frat brothers. You know, the people who loved me the most. They would witness me jumping the broom, tying the knot, and all the other clever colloquialisms that people say when someone is committing to spend the rest of their lives with the love of their life. This day was the beginning of a life full of love, happiness, and unrestricted sex. Dude, you know a brother was ready.

However, I must admit that I was extremely nervous and yet in the same breath, I was absolutely clueless about what I was really saying "I do" to. In all honesty, this was a day I thought I might not ever see, because the bachelor in me never really wanted to commit to one woman.

My father raised me by himself after my grandmother, who we lived with, passed away. I grew up seeing him date different women, all the time. Through hearsay, I also found out that my grandfather (his father) did the same thing – and he was a married man.

I actually enjoyed being a single brother. I was also having a lot of fun hanging out with the ladies in Washington DC, AKA

Chocolate City. Man, I love chocolate. Milk chocolate. Special Dark, etc. Was I really about to give all of this up for one woman? A woman who had a child?

Anyway, back to the story – the big moment arrived. There she was, my beautiful bride. She looked amazing with the blue sky overhead and birds chirping. She was escorted down a grassy aisle with her father by her side. He was giving her to me.

Me – that guy who had no idea how to be a husband or even what a husband was. On top of that, little did I know, he was not just giving me his daughter, but I was getting all of her quirks, and all of her bills, along with the other things that would soon get on my last good nerve.

When I think back on it, it is wild how I ignored all of those things when we were dating. Yes, she was bossy as hell, but I liked that in the women I dated. She was super independent, extremely organized, and did I mention she had pretty toes and a 'phat' booty?

I did think that she was a bit obsessive with her house cleaning and how everything had to be in its rightful place. But I didn't give those things too much energy, even though they were right there in my face in High Definition.

She was different from the other women I'd messed with in the past and I liked that. Man, those same things would soon be the bane of my existence. I had no idea I was in for a rude awakening.

My soon-to-be wife also had a seven-year-old daughter who I would immediately be one hundred percent responsible for upon uttering two words: "I do." I was inheriting a real, live daughter. This dynamic would shift me from months of being "Mr. Don" to Daddy instantly. I would be the daddy of a little girl who had her own needs as well.

I was cool with being Mr. Don. It fitted me. But this dad thing was a little overwhelming for me. I really thought I was good leading up to the wedding but standing there looking at Gabi come down the aisle with her basket of lilac roses, throwing them on the runner, made me nervous. What was I about to do? This just got really REAL.

I also had the realization that I didn't have the standard nine-month waiting period to warm up to the idea of being a new parent. I knew I was going to be a daddy, but it just didn't click until I saw her bright smile looking up at me. My immediate thought was, "BAM, you're a dad to a child. A child who has to get used to seeing you and interacting with you every single day of her life."

I know you are thinking, "Did you guys go to marriage counseling before the big day?" The answer is "Yes, we did. We went for the required six weeks." The pastor, who conducted our marriage counseling, was a great guy and we loved him and his wife. However, I don't remember him educating me on any of pertinent issues, like dealing with our past or what to do when your wife is bossy as hell.

We didn't talk about my wife's baby daddy, what to do if either of us became unemployed, resolving healthy conflict resolution, or all the other things we argued about for the first thirteen years of marriage.

If he did, I must have been asleep for that session, because I would have been the first one to object to all the above and more. I really didn't understand marriage was that serious. I know that may sound crazy to you. Don't judge me. At that time, it truly was logical – to me.

Marriage was like being boyfriend and girlfriend, on paper and for forever. I guess I wanted what I wanted, which was my wife, but I truly didn't know what I was getting. I would venture to say most of us are clueless going into marriage.

Okay, where was I? Oh yeah, so our very beautiful wedding was all I could imagine it was going to be from a guy's point of view. Our honeymoon was all but one night. By the next morning, it was over. After all, it consisted of dinner at the Baltimore Inner Harbor and we spent our wedding night at the Sheraton. We didn't even have a room facing the water.

The next morning, we were in the car repeating "wow" about one hundred times as well as saying the words "husband" and "wife" over and again. When we got back to the house, it was the door to our new reality. Husband and wife, mom and dad. Yo, that is deep.

This was a world that I will confess, I had no real clue about how to operate in. Raise your hand if you woke up one day and wondered, "How the hell did I get here?" If you are honest, I'm sure you've done that rather frequently. I know I did almost weekly for years. At that time, there were no marriage boot camps. If there were, I didn't know about them. I just thought you get married and life is great.

My parents were divorced, and I have no memory of them being together. Because they were divorced when I was very young, I do not remember us being a family. I just remember doing the house shuffle from my mother's house in North Philly to my father's in Chester County, PA.

That's where he lived with my grandmother who helped raise me. My great-grandparents were married for about seventy years or close to it, but I was too young to really understand the love that they had for each other.

Thinking back on those early days of my marriage, I realize I was struggling in my attempt to adjust to having a wife and a daughter, in what appeared to be in the blink of an eye.

It was like I closed my eyes and opened them to this new world of responsibilities and things that I never had to do or even considered. Anyone who knows me knows I am a trooper, so I was up for the challenge – or so I thought.

I knew Vedia and I were a little different from each other and had polar opposite upbringings. But I thought our differences would work themselves out and that we would be on the same sheet of music sooner rather than later.

Little did I know that I had a full-blown independent woman who was not willing to share the stage of marriage with anyone, not even her husband. In her world, it was her way or no way.

This was a major culture shock for me. This would be my first time living with a woman. I had never shared my personal space with anyone since college. I found out quickly that when you are married, there is no personal space – it's our space.

Yes, deciding who got what space in the house was problematic. She had already mapped out a space for everything in the house and I had no say in it. I had a lot of learning to do and I had to do it quick. There were no CliffsNotes for reading the Mrs. Vedia Barnett.

Now, fellas, we all know that the toilet seat stays in 'the up position" unless we need to take a seat and get some things off our mind. Who knew that you had to put the toilet seat down so your wife doesn't fall in it in the middle of the night? I sure didn't know or consider it until my wife fell into the toilet in the middle of the night. Trust me, it never, ever happened again.

The other part of being married I did not consider is that I would have to be home at a respectable time. This is something we never discussed before getting married. Man, I wish we had. That would have saved a lot of heated arguments at three o'clock in the morning.

We also had quite a few of what I would like to consider as some early growing pains. Okay, brother, you got me. I'm lying. We had full-blown, funky, cussing-Christian arguments. You can imagine my initial reaction when all hell broke loose in my marriage.

I literally wanted to do a Carl Lewis and Usain Bolt out the back door and never come back. I was not mentally or emotionally prepared to cope with this new wife I had. She wasn't equipped to cope with the husband she had. We were straight up busted.

Yeah, she was cute, sexy, and forever caring but man, when we did not agree on something, this chick was on some different stuff. Need I say more, the single-man mindset I had, tapped me on my shoulder and told me I didn't need to put up with her bull. You already know: we were going nowhere fast. I was never taught that you could have differences in marriage.

No one prepared me to not get along with my wife. Instead of me being the love of her life, I found myself being her enemy and vice versa. We got along great when we were dating – all of six months, I might add.

We had sex all the time. Like for real, all the time. However, this marriage thing changed the game up. We simply could not see eye to eye after saying "I do" and it seemed like the sex well dried up soon after the exchanging of our vows. She was still a lady in the streets, but the freak never showed up in my bedroom. I was so over being a husband!

We also argued all the time. We couldn't even agree about what to eat for dinner. Who does that? MY LOVELY BRAND-NEW WIFE, that's who. I grew up just being thankful to have something to eat.

There was no way in hell I was going to debate with my grandmother, Ruth Barnett, about what she was fixing to eat and survive that encounter. I loved my life too much to try that. I'm sure you probably grew up the same way.

My wife, on the other hand, was used to a meat, a starch, a vegetable, napkins, and the occasional red Kool-Aid in a real glass, if she a had good day at school. That was her expectation for our marriage. She was not trying to eat on paper plates with plastic utensils. Dude, we were from two opposite worlds.

Because money was scarce when I was growing up, I was raised knowing how to make do with what we had in the refrigerator. I grew up eating spaghetti mixed in the sauce in the same pot. We ate a lot of one-pot meals in my childhood. This, I quickly learned, was all foreign to my wife.

She grew up with her spaghetti noodles and sauce prepared separately, with a pretty bowl of salad with radishes, croutons, and red onions on top, piping hot garlic bread and a glass of icy cold milk. She was rich in my eyes.

When we first got married, my wife did the bulk of the cooking. Then I threw my hat in the ring to assist my wife with dinner duty. I wanted to fix quick meals in a pinch. I felt like I was doing it big when I made Hamburger Helper.

And you clearly could not tell me I was not a chef when I prepared beans and hot dogs and other quick, high-sodium and high-fat meals. I really felt this was an appropriate dinner, since that's what I ate growing up. In her home, beans and hot dogs were lunch food, not dinner food. She let me know that really quick too, with her bougie self.

I was seriously confused a few weeks after our wedding. How could two people who seemed to be so much alike be so different? How do I, as a husband and man, deal with this woman? These are some questions I asked myself early in my marriage because I didn't have to deal with any of these behaviors when I was single, or even when I was dating her.

Initially, this marriage was all fun and games. But before I knew it, marriage was extremely draining very early on. It felt like my helpmeet, my wife, my best friend, had turned into an enemy combatant and I was not prepared for this war.

Slowly but surely, I tried to adjust to this new lifestyle and new way of living and doing things. I did my very best not to make mountains out of molehills, but this chick was getting on my last nerves.

This being the head of the house stuff was and still is not easy. In church, they make it all sound real simple. "Men, you should be the head of your household," they say. Well, they never met my wife, all her mouth, and all of her attitude.

She acted like she was the head of our household and like I was a kid. I must own that I would sometimes ignore her simply to just have peace in my house. In those instances, I allowed her to reign like a queen instead of having a mature discussion about my feelings. I was drowning and did not know how to come up out of this.

I noticed that oftentimes, men pretend like we got this. I ask you, "Do we really? Why don't we ask for help when we clearly are in over our heads? Why do we suffer alone?" I was racking my brain with things I felt a husband should do, but I had no real point of reference.

So, what was I supposed to do? You already know: I faked it. I faked at church, at work, and even with my homies. My friends and frat brothers, for the most part, did not know that I had drama in my house. I had no one to be real and honest with about my struggles.

I had no idea how I was going to remain married to Ve. I was slowly falling out of love with her, but I couldn't tell anybody since we were newlyweds. How would that look?

I used to ask my father-in-law roundabout questions to find out how he had done this husband thing for so long. I was happy that he and I got along and that he treated me like a son. I had to be strategic though, because I didn't want him to think I was being too critical about his daughter, my wife.

He had always been easy going with a laid-back mentality like my father had when dealing with me. I wanted to love my wife in an easy going way too, but I was clueless and in need of guidance. At that time, my in-laws had been married well into forty-something years. They are still married today and will be celebrating their fiftieth anniversary in a few years.

I could tell Vedia wanted me to be so much like her father. That if she could, I'm certain she would have swapped my brain for his and then programmed it just right to fit her needs. She used to make constant remarks like, "My daddy doesn't do that," or "This is how my daddy would do it." That could be something as simple as cutting the grass.

With only a few weeks in our marriage, it felt like I'd heard her say "My daddy …" 1000 times already. That is a blower for a man who is doing the best he can with what he has. I knew her dad was a good man, but I had no clue how to be a husband.

My wife found out she was pregnant a few months after we got married. I was on cloud nine. I was going to finally be a father to my own child. Even though we had Gabi, I wanted a child of my own too. Everyone was excited when I told them I was finally going to be a father. I just knew things would get better for me and my wife, since we were expecting a baby.

Well, things didn't get better. On the contrary, we were on a downward spiral.

About two months into her pregnancy, Ve started having terrible morning sickness. I was immediately stuck doing everything.

The smell of food kept her in the bathroom all day long. She went from having morning sickness to having morning, noon, and night sickness. At one point she could only keep down Welch's Grape Popsicles and Chipwich ice cream sandwiches.

I was at 7-11 almost weekly, stocking up on those ice cream sandwiches. I'm sure you are thinking, "Wow, her pregnancy must have been a blessing in disguise and they finally chilled out." Nope, it did not decrease our arguments; they intensified.

Eventually, the stress from arguing all the time sent my wife to the hospital with Braxton Hicks contractions. We visited Labor and Delivery three to four different times, with her being in premature labor each time. Her doctor feared for the baby, so she finally admitted Ve for an entire week.

It was truly a miserable existence for the both of us. Everything that could go wrong in pregnancy happened to my wife. I was not ready for any of it.

During one of her hospitalizations, they had my wife was in the hospital bed upside down so the baby would not put pressure on her cervix. They drugged her to the max to keep her from contracting. I felt helpless and so scared. But I could do nothing. I had to go to work and I had to take care of Gabi.

It was crazy. I did not sign up for this. I was worried about two lives: my wife and that of our unborn baby. This was about the most stressful thing either of us had experienced since being married.

One day, my wife asked me to bring a CD player to the hospital, so she could at least have some music to listen to. We loved the group Men of Standard. "Yet Will I Trust in Him" was her song, so I set that CD on repeat for days. That song was the only prayer she could utter because of the drugs she was given. That song still brings tears to our eyes when we hear it.

The drugs were so strong that she was in and out of consciousness for hours at a time. I looked forward to visiting and sitting with her after working a full day. I prayed for the life of our baby. We asked God to spare the baby's life and to bring us closer during this craziness.

I think this was the first time we prayed together for a common thing. All we had at that point was prayer and each other. We also had to be patient and trust God to keep this baby from being born prematurely.

A week later, my wife was discharged from the hospital. She was not allowed to do anything. She was on one hundred percent bedrest. Everything was on me. I did not know what to do. I was in shock from the amount of responsibility resting on my shoulders.

We clearly were not hip to this in pre-marriage counseling. I was not sure if I had what it took to be a good husband and now, I was not sure if I would be ready for this new baby we were praying for.

Even after she got home, she was still on me. The straw that broke the camel's back was the grass incident. Her dad came to visit us a few weeks after she was discharged from the hospital.

Because I was working all the time and worrying about her pregnancy, cutting the damn grass was the last thing on my mind. I did not care that the grass looked like the meadow out of *Little House on the Prairie*. I would get to the grass when I found the time to get to it and when I was ready to cut it.

Well, don't you know, Little Miss "My Daddy" decided to cut our overgrown grass; while she was on bedrest. Yes, you read right. My wife was on bedrest for premature labor. To make matters worse, this all happened while I was at work.

Little did I know, when her dad got to the house, he commented on how nice the grass looked and that he was proud of ME for keeping the yard up. Because my wife used to be Petty Patty, she took the opportunity to make me look bad in front of her dad.

She proudly boasted that she, in fact, had cut the grass. She explained that she HAD TO do it because I didn't see it as a priority. She was ready for her dad to be angry at me because she had to cut the grass.

Needless to say, that backfired on her terribly. Her dad went off on her. He was so upset with her because she put her pregnancy in danger because the stupid grass was not cut.

Now, I had no idea all this transpired because like I said, I was at work. When I got home, I assumed my father-in-law had cut the grass, simply because he's that type of guy. I love that dude. I went to thank him for generously cutting our grass after traveling to see us. Imagine my surprise when I found out that my wife was the one who had cut the grass.

I cursed her out one side and down the other for taking such a crazy risk, just because she wanted the grass cut when she wanted it cut. Her rationale was that she was tired of asking me to do stuff around the house only for me to blow her off. She was trying to get even with me. She was testing my manhood.

I told her straight up that I did not appreciate the fact that she'd thrown me under the bus in front of her dad. She saw nothing wrong with it since, in her mind, I should have already cut the grass anyway. We didn't talk for a few days after that.

We'd already had several arguments surrounding yard work, housework, meal prep, and the grass being cut. We were in trouble, but I had no idea how to fix it. But, I knew: her trying to change me into someone and something I was not would be counterproductive.

I just didn't know how to vocalize it at the time, so lashing out at her was my only way to express myself. I own that, way back then, I should have sought help, but it never crossed my mind. I just felt like I was trapped in this miserable abyss called marriage.

A few months later, my wife was admitted to the hospital again. She was given more drugs to stop the contractions. That time, instead of camping out beside my wife's hospital bed, I had to go to work every day. I was devastated and stressed out.

When I did visit, my wife and I would sit there going back and forth from looking at each other and to the baby monitor, terrified. The baby monitor produced unending waves of contractions.

My wife was in so much pain and I could do nothing but watch helplessly. A nurse checked my wife and told us that her cervix was indeed opening and that she was at two centimeters. She apologized to us and said the baby was coming at twenty-two weeks. I watch someone create baby bands.

They started prepping my wife for the delivery of our baby. She was crying. I had never seen my wife cry up to this point in our relationship. That's how I knew she was really scared. She knew a baby born at that stage would not survive. I grabbed my wife's hand and prayed. We declared that this baby would not be born prematurely.

The neonatal and pediatric staffs came in to talk to us about what to expect once the baby was born. They informed us of the fact that the baby probably would not survive. Ve was given a shot of a steroid to mature the baby's lungs, in hopes that it would prevent its lungs from collapsing at birth.

The radiology team also came in to perform a last-minute sonogram. At that moment, we found out the baby was a girl. I told my wife that we needed to pray using the name we'd chosen for her, Donielle Jahnaé Barnett. We asked God to stop the labor.

I kid you not, within twenty-four hours of all the preparation for the delivery of our baby girl, my wife's contractions stopped.

The medical team was amazed. Even though we knew it was the direct result of our praying together, we were still shocked to see that it had worked.

My wife was discharged about a week later with doctor's orders of bedrest again. However, true to form, we were back to arguing and fussing with each other just a few days later. My wife had several more hospital visits for premature labor throughout that pregnancy.

A few weeks before her due date, Ve had a terrible cough that would not go away after several doctor's appointments. I took her to the emergency room for another opinion. The x-rays showed she had a terrible case of pneumonia, so back to Labor and Delivery we went. They admitted her and gave her IV antibiotics. Her doctor chose to induce her labor instead of having her go back and forth to the hospital any more.

I watched my wife experience three days of intense labor. Then she woke up with a one-hundred-three-degree fever. She looked at me and said that she felt like something was wrong.

They called her doctor because her pain was no longer relieved by the epidural. When her doctor finally got to the hospital, she checked her and then rushed Ve to the operating room.

My baby girl, Donielle, was born at 37 weeks via an emergency Caesarean section. We found out later that the pain my wife felt was because her placenta was coming apart from her uterus due, to being in labor for three days. I had no idea this had created a life-or-death situation for the both of them.

Once we were settled at home, life was great again. My wife and I were in love with each other and this new baby. Gabi enjoyed being a big sister and helping with the baby too. Even though I was excited about this new baby and all life had to offer, I oftentimes wondered, "What did I do? I did not sign up for all of this."

Ask Yourself:

- When was the last time you had a serious conversation with yourself about your life?
- How many times have you said or done something you wished you could erase or take back?
- How many times have you felt misunderstood by the people you love?
- How did that make you feel?
- How many times have you felt misunderstood by the woman you love/d?
- Were you ever comfortable speaking your truth to her/them? Why or why not?
- When was the last time you had a heart to heart conversation with her/them?

Instant Replay: Notes to myself

2 You Said He's Just A Friend

"There is no better than adversity. Every defeat, every heartbreak, every loss, contains its own seed, its own lesson on how to improve your performance next time."

Malcolm X

One day, early in our marriage, I was home getting some rest while Vedia was still at work. The phone rang and there was a dude on the other line asking to speak to my wife. This guy clearly was not a bill collector calling for her. I know what those sound like. My husband radar went off. I not so nicely asked him who the hell he was.

He went on to explain that he was a family friend or some other bullcrap. He said he heard that she had gotten married and that he was calling to congratulate her. My blood immediately began to boil on the inside because I had never heard her say this person's name. I thought to myself, "Why is this guy really calling my wife?" We exchanged niceties and hung up, but this was far from over.

When my wife came home, the first thing out my mouth was not, "Hey baby doll, how was your day?" No sir, it was more like, "Who the blankety-blank is this guy? How did he get our number? Why did he call our house?" She said, "Babe, he's just a friend." She "reminded" me that he'd always had this number because it was her parents' number.

I reminded her that we no longer had her parents' number since we had moved into their vacant house after our wedding. I rationalized that she had to have talked to him at some point and given the new number to him. She denied this profusely, but I was not trying to hear it.

"Exiting stage right," "deuces," "peace out," "bouncing," and "bailing" were the only things on my mind at the time. Since she was already starting to get on my nerves, I figured this would be my way out of this marriage.

The more I thought about it, the more I rationalized my wife was still messing with this dude. I decided to pack my clothes. A brother was on his way out the door and out of this rotten marriage. She clearly was not the woman I fell in love with.

My wife was crying uncontrollably but at the time, I did not have it in me to care. With tears in her eyes, she grabbed my duffel bag and begged me to stay. She said repeatedly that he was just a friend from high school.

I was willing to give her a chance to redeem herself with my next question. I chose to go hard so I asked the ultimate question, "Did you ever sleep with him?" She looked at me like a deer in headlights. With fear in her voice, she barely croaked out, "No".

You already know I didn't believe her, but I said, "Okay," anyway and chilled out to buy me some time. Even though I was boiling on the inside because I just knew she was lying, I played it cool like Billy Dee Williams in a Colt 45 commercial. I remembered my grandmother always said, "Son, what is done in the dark will come to light".

Since I could tell my wife wanted to move on from the conversation, I let it go. Plus, I couldn't prove anything, yet.

Being as though I had a bachelor's degree in Criminal Justice, I made a choice to turn into John Shaft, the black 1970s detective. I just could not let it go. It was eating away at me. When I just couldn't take it anymore, I decided to do some searching. You know that other old saying: "You go looking for something, you just might find it?" Your boy did that very thing.

Well, well, well... I stumbled across a trunk that was my wife's from her college days. I was in luck too; it was unlocked. I am not going to fake and lie to you and say I was thinking, "What would Jesus do?"

Nah, bruh, I turned into a CSI officer who was looking for hard, cold evidence. This was so unlike me and for a hot second, I wanted to stop. But I didn't. Something was moving me forward. I simply had to find out the truth.

I shuffled through Ve's posters and all her New Edition fan paraphernalia. This woman had items from high school, lots of photos, and even some items dating back to elementary school. I was thinking that this chick was a pack rat or lowkey hoarder.

Then, suddenly, BINGO! I came across the prize. The Prize, you might ask? The prize was her diary. I know, I know... you're thinking, "Did this grown man really read his wife's diary?"

Sadly, I did. I sat on the basement floor reading my wife's diary like I was one of those middle school brothers you see on television invading his big sister's privacy. It didn't take me long to find the proof I was looking for about *Mr. Telephone Man*.

There it was, in her pink swirly handwriting with hearts, stars, and stickers. Even though the entries were from back in the day and it was now 1999, I found what I was looking for. I was vindicated, and I was going to make her pay for lying to me. As I sat there fuming, I was dumbfounded that she lied to my face so easily.

I didn't care that she was frightened by my earlier yelling and cursing at her. All I cared about was proving her to be a *trick* and finding a reason to finally get a divorce. I got angrier and angrier as I looked for more juicy information. I found it, page after page.

Pissed off, I went upstairs to confront her with evidence in hand. All the color drained from her face when she saw what I was holding. Once again, I could not contain myself, so I started kirking out. I was so angry and was shouting all sorts of things in her direction.

I am not talking about the kind of shouting we do in church. Oh no, I am talking about the kind that is loud, and involves explicit language and name calling. I hate that I did this to her and it was neither the first nor the last time.

Looking back, I am not proud of my behavior. I really should have handled this better. However, had she simply been honest when I initially questioned her, I would like to think that I would have handled this a little better.

I don't believe in holding things against people that happened before you knew them. In my mind, if someone lies about a relationship with the opposite sex, it implies that they are still involved in that very thing they are trying to hide. The moral of this story is to tell the truth, no matter what.

At that moment, I felt that the trust I had for my new wife had been violated and broken. This made the puzzle (marriage) that I was trying to piece together that much more complicated. My initial feelings of trying to figure out how to be a husband were just about gone and I felt overwhelmed with it all.

Let's be clear, if this incident had happened when we were dating, she would have been yesterday's news. I would have moved on from her like I had done with so many other women before her for lesser infractions.

Regret, and the feeling of being trapped in a situation I no longer felt I wanted to be in, started to creep into my mind. The truth of the matter is I was hurt and didn't know how to deal with those emotions other than running away and wanting to find someone else to fill that void. I didn't see this thought process as a problem at the time. I believed that if I divorced my wife, I had every right because she had betrayed me.

I also rationalized that because my father was divorced and his father before him, along with many of my other family members, that getting a divorce would be no big deal. They weren't bad people, they just married the wrong person. I felt that I must have married the wrong person too.

It wasn't until I went to counseling years later that I found out my reason for feeling betrayed stemmed out of my mother never keeping her word when I was younger. I held my wife to this same standard and because she lied to me, I placed her in that same space as my absentee mother.

For years, I held my wife in this place until I received therapy. Therapy allowed me to address those thoughts and free my wife from this prison.

Ask Yourself:

- Have you ever been hurt by someone else's lies?
- How did you handle it?
- Were you ever caught in a lie/ lies?
- How did you handle this?
- Did you ever get away with lies?
- How does knowing this make you feel today?
- Who do you need to forgive that hurt you by their lies?
- Whose forgiveness do you need to seek?

Instant Replay: Notes to myself

3 If Only My Dad Had Been There

"You may not control all the events that happen to you, but you can decide not to be reduced by them." Maya Angelou

A few years into this thing called marriage, I was no longer having any fun. I was looking at the end of my enlistment in the army and was still trying to find a way to cope with my life and my wife. My wife had given birth to our son while we lived in Germany. I looked forward to seeing him and the girls when I got off my twelve-hour shifts.

During that time, we were both sleep deprived and our young daughters were getting to the age where they could feel when daddy was frustrated. This frustration led to more arguments with my wife. I was so tired of the issues in my marriage. If only my dad had been there, I would have had someone to talk to.

My dad was just simply that dude for me. My dad was always there no matter what things looked like. He loved me unconditionally. He always made a way for me to do and to have the things I wanted. He also kept it real with me before that became trendy. I remember my dad telling me one day, "Boy, if you get a girl pregnant, you can't go to college. You'll have to get a job and work the rest of your life because of the kid."

Looking back on it, that was my dad's way of saying, "Don't have sex or if you do, use protection." That was one of many Mr. Miyagi-type talks we had when I was growing up. I sure could have used those talks in the early years of my marriage and fatherhood.

I didn't know what to do with a wife who I was constantly in a cat and dog fight with. I never saw my dad argue with my mother because she was not around. Come to think of it, I never saw my dad argue with anyone at all.

I remember growing up and hearing my dad telling me things like "Never hit a woman," and "Son, if you find things getting heated with a woman, just walk away." He stressed that point to me all the time. I later learned that my grandfather – his father, who I never knew – allegedly physically abused my grandmother. I think this is the reason why my dad was very adamant about me keeping my hands to myself no matter what happened in a relationship.

In all honesty, I can say that keeping my hands to myself was never an issue but controlling what came out of my mouth? Yeah, that was a real big problem. At the time, I was accustomed to just blowing up when I was pissed off. Looking back on it, it was definitely something I needed to work on when attempting to communicate.

I own that I have used plenty of foul language when arguing with my wife. I also own that I have withheld emotional support and love from my wife, on purpose. If only my dad had been there, I would have been a more peaceful and loving husband.

You see, my father always had a way of making things make sense to me. He was always calm when he spoke to me. He was also my sounding board and my voice of reason. My dad was the one person in my life who could tell me the proper course of action regardless of my situation. Even though he and my mother divorced when I was a little kid, I am sure he could have offered me something positive to use in my marriage like only he could.

I can envision him now, sitting in his recliner, watching television, dropping nuggets of knowledge on me about life and being a young man. I would give anything in the world to have had even just one of those talks after I got married. He always took lemons and made lemonade with his big smile and sense of humor.

My dad wasn't there because he died when I was a teenager. It was a time in my life when I needed him the most. When he passed away, I didn't just lose my father, I lost my best friend. He was my "ride or die" homie. I really missed my dad in those early years of marriage and I could have really used his man-to-man talks.

I can only imagine what my dad would have thought if he knew my wife and I argued all the time, like neither one of us had any home training. I'm sure he would have been disappointed that his only son was not mature enough to be the bigger person to end the confusion in his home and in his marriage. Maybe if he had been there, I would have been a different man – a man who loved his wife and himself unconditionally.

I often play back in my mind the various conversations my dad and I had. It feels like it was just yesterday that we were chatting it up. Unfortunately, none of those conversations covered how to be a good husband.

I have looked for father figures to somehow fill the void, but no one could ever take my dad's place. Out of all the things in life that my dad taught me and showed me how to do, none of them covered the things I wish I'd known before I said, "I do."

But at the end of it all, I could not blame my shortcomings and poor behavior on the fact that my father was not there anymore. I had to take ownership of all of it. If my dad had been there, I could have gone to him for advice, but the choices would still have been mine to make.

Ask Yourself:

- Do you still blame your childhood or life circumstances for where you are in life?
- Have you made excuses for 'kirking out'?
- What could you have done instead that is productive
- What can you do in the future if a situation arises that would ease that?
- Have you allowed pain and disappointment to cloud your judgement?
- When was the last time you apologized for your poor choices or damaging words that hurt others?

Instant Replay: Notes to myself

4 Dear Mama

If you enter this world knowing you are loved and you leave this world knowing the same, then everything that happens in between can be dealt with. Michael Jackson

Have you ever heard that old saying, "The way a man treats his mother is how he will treat you?" Well, I never really believed that saying but after looking back on my life, I would have to say: there is some truth to that.

My mother and I don't have a relationship. For as long as I can remember, she was in and out of my life throughout my childhood. I still remember as a child, I was shuffled from my mother's house and then back to my dad's house.

One day, I noticed that the trips back and forth started becoming few and far in between. The visits then became just a phone call, then those phone calls became sporadic. There were times in my life where the visits were so scarce that a year or so would go by without me seeing or hearing from my mother.

I remember talking to my mother on the phone, with tears in my eyes, asking, "Mommy, are you coming to get me tomorrow?" She would assure me that she was coming. The next day, I would run to look out the window whenever I heard a car drive by, thinking it was her.

Eventually, I would fall asleep on my grandma's sofa near that very window. I would wake up in my dad's room a few hours later, devastated that once again, she didn't come to get me.

I was on an emotional roller coaster of love and hate with my mother to the point where I just became numb. I just didn't care about her anymore. The little ray of hope I had for reconciliation went away when my father passed away.

I had just graduated from high school two months prior to his death. I have never felt so much pain in my life. My grandma had died years earlier and her death crushed me. Losing my father took everything out of me. I could not think straight. I could barely breathe.

I found myself in a perpetual state of confusion. I was constantly asking myself, "What am I going to do? Where am I going to go? How am I going to survive without him?"

I had one glimmer of hope regarding my mother after my father died. I toyed with the idea that my mother was going to come in like an African Queen and save her warrior prince son to guide him and teach him how to be a man. It was nothing like that.

There was one instant where she did come through and it was the nicest thing she has ever done for me in my life. I was in the home stretch of my senior year at Lincoln University. I owed the bursar's office $700. If I didn't pay it, I could've been in jeopardy of not graduating. I had a phone conversation with my mother one day and she asked me how I was doing. I don't know what made me tell her that I needed that money.

To my surprise, she said she would be at my school the next day to pay it. Just like all the other times in the past, I blew it off. Imagine my surprise when my line brother said there was a lady at the door who said she was my mother. I quickly got dressed to see if it was true. I almost passed out when I saw her. I even asked her what she was doing here.

She repeated she was there to pay my remaining tuition, so I could graduate on time. I could not believe she was there in flesh and blood. To this day, that was the last thing she ever did for me.

Why am I sharing this with you? Because I never really knew how much my mother's absence in my life affected me until I took a real look in the mirror a few years ago. I thought about all the relationships or one-night-stands I had with women who I had easily dismissed because something they did or said reminded me too much of my mother.

I was very guarded and wasn't going to let anyone hurt me like she did. I think about how I found comfort with these women because they were there at my leisure and pleasure. When they weren't around, I felt lonely and rejected. These feelings motivated me to find other women who would avail themselves to me whenever I called.

The truth of the matter is I was damaged goods. I went from woman to woman looking for happiness, peace, and even love. I had no clue that I was emotionally hurting these women in the process of searching for love.

Years later, I realized that no matter what any of these women did for me, it just wouldn't be enough to satisfy me. I had to face the fact that until I settled the issues regarding my mother, I could never heal.

In the past, I had tried to talk things out with my mother, but I never got anywhere. For some reason, these conversations turned into the blame game. She always put the blame on everyone else, including yours truly. After all, I believed that she should have tried to work things out with me because I was her son. She never took ownership of anything. I will never understand this no matter how hard I try.

My issues with my mother clearly affected my relationship with my wife. For years, several arguments my wife and I had sometimes played out in front of my kids. My wife would ask me to chill but I couldn't. I just kept going in, even though the kids may have been right there.

It eventually got to a point where my wife suggested, for the one-hundredth time, that I seek therapy. I realized that I just couldn't allow these issues regarding my mother to affect us anymore.

I finally wanted to be healed and free from the pain of my mother not giving a damn about me and now my kids, her grandchildren. I wanted the hate I had in my heart for my mother to be gone forever. I wanted to stop blaming my wife for the stuff my mother did and did not do.

One Sunday, I finally settled the issue with my mother. I know you're probably thinking we had a sit-down conversation and hugged it out. That is not even close to what happened. You see, on that Sunday, when I went to church, the pastor's message was about honor. He spoke about how you need to honor your parents, regardless of what they had done or had not done in your life.

In my head, I was thinking, "You haven't met my mother." I wanted to receive the message, but I just could not accept that he wanted me to honor a person who didn't even think about me. He went on to talk about how the lack of honor for one's parents affects everything you do.

At the end of his message, he did an altar call to pray for people dealing with whatever issues they may have had concerning honor or the lack thereof. I stayed in my seat at first but then I felt the Holy Spirit, along with what felt like my wife's foot in my back, pushing me to the altar.

Side note: I do not want to lose any of you brothers who are not Christians – I am simply sharing the experience I had which began my healing process.

I must be extremely transparent with you in this moment: I have been to the altar numerous times and to all sorts of prayer groups concerning my relationship with my mother. I had been doing this for as long as I can remember, but this time, I felt something different happen to me.

The pastor came to me as I stood at the altar. I told him why I was there, and he said he was going to pray for me. I guess I was a bad case, because he called in for some reinforcements.

He and another minister placed their hands on me as he began to pray. I felt years of pain and hate for my mother begin to leave my heart. That was not the end, though. This guy then asked me to verbally say, "I love you, mama."

I immediately looked at him and, in my mind, I asked him, "You want me to what?" At that moment, I had a decision to make. I didn't want to utter those four words. I cannot tell you the last time I said them.

Since I wanted to be totally free of carrying around this weight, I decided to trust the pastor and the process. To be clear, this was not easy. I was warring within myself. I did not want to say those words, but I just did not want to leave the altar, once again, carrying the same burdens back to my seat.

I've been to the altar way too many times in my adult life. Even though I would always lay this same burden down, I always picked it back up and took them back home again.

With tears running down my face, my mouth tried to form the words. I was conflicted. How could I say these words out loud? How can I replace my hate with love for my mother? How could I love my mother who didn't even love me?

I took my head out of the decision and chose to act with my heart. Then it happened. I actually said, "I love you mama and I forgive you."

I said those words as though she was standing right there in front of me. I bawled my eyes out as I allowed God's love to fill me. I went back to my seat, knowing this issue was truly settled. I could go forward no longer allowing myself to feel like a victim. I was victorious, and I had the love of my wife and children, as well as God's love, to sustain me.

Brother, I wish I could tell you my mother and I now talk daily or that we see each other every weekend. I wish I could say that she is a fantastic grandmother and great-grandmother. Unfortunately, she is not. How can she be, if she doesn't keep in contact with me or come around?

She could literally walk up to my kids and they would not know who she is. But I no longer hold this against her. After all, she is the one missing out on all that our lives have to offer. At the end of the day, I am still praying for her. I pray that one day she will decide to be a part of our lives.

Ask Yourself:

- What past hurts are you are holding onto?
- Do you need to forgive your parent(s) for hurting you?
- Who do you need to forgive?
- Is there a way you can forgive them right now even though they may not be in your presence, like I did?
- Who have you hurt and need to ask for their forgiveness?
- How would your life improve if you asked for forgiveness?

Instant Replay: Notes to myself

5 I Don't Want To Go Home

It is not a lack of love, but a lack of friendship that makes unhappy marriages.
Friedrich Nietzsche

I'm sure you are wondering, "What in the world would make a forty-something-year-old, 250lb grown-ass man not want to go home his wife and their three wonderful children?" There is only one answer: a 5'1" woman with the attitude and bark of a rabid pit-bull with a Porterhouse steak dangling in front of it on the end of a stick.

Even though my wife was a loving woman to everyone else, she did not cut me any breaks. None! Zero! Nada! Nunca! She expected me to be perfect, all the time. Remember the grass cutting incident? Well, she was like that with everything. She challenged my manhood often.

There were times when I felt so emotionally and mentally weak after dealing with her. I felt like a trapped animal whenever we had a heated conversation. She would follow me from room to room, so she could get her point out, even though I would yell at her to leave me alone.

My wife couldn't wait to hand over the duties of taking care of my children the minute I walked through the door. She was waiting with whatever she had on that to-do list from H-E-Double-Hockey-Sticks! Seriously, a brother could not catch a break.

Because of this, I wouldn't have any time to decompress from my hectic workday, nor from the long drive home in traffic. Don't let it rain – my one-hour commute would easily convert to a two to three-hour nightmare. Since my job was stressful, I just needed a few minutes to chill when I got home.

Most times, when I walked in the door, I wouldn't even get a "Hey, babe, how was your day?" It was more like: "Whew! Finally, you are home. I need you to…" You can already guess that this caused many heated arguments, none of which I really had the energy to participate in after a long day.

I believe home is supposed to be a place of refuge and a place where you can just unwind and relax from the cares of your day with your family. My home, at the time, was anything but a place of refuge. I hated going home. It felt like a plantation.

My wife acted like she was the overseer from *Roots*, standing ready to verbally beat me down for not following "the rules," which were her rules. In Proverbs 21:19, it says, "Better to dwell in the wilderness than with a contentious and angry woman." Let's just say, at one point, a brotha was tent shopping.

We had a lot going on at that time. It also made our relationship ridiculously volatile. Looking back on it, I realized she needed a break too. She was operating a home daycare, working on completing her bachelor's degree, homeschooling our two youngest kids, coaching cheer, and the list goes on.

She was the captain of Team-Do-Too-Much and it negatively affected our marriage. All the things my wife was doing were great things, it was just too much, and our relationship suffered because of it.

To prepare myself for what I had to deal with when I walked in the door, I used to find any reason to go to Happy Hour with the fellas. The Happy Hour spot was on my way home and it usually began at three.

It was the perfect diversion for me. I faithfully got off work at two and unbeknownst to my wife, I would dip off there for a few minutes for drinks and simply to unwind.

This was the break I longed for and desperately needed at the end of my day. Talking with the fellas, the bartenders, and even some of the women there gave me the release I needed before crossing the threshold of Casa de Barnett.

I loved talking to people and I felt real chill sitting there shooting the breeze with the fellas. I also didn't see anything wrong with it because, hey, everybody else was there too. This also dulled the irritation of walking in the door and seeing my wife.

After my Happy Hour stop, my wife would simply sound like the teacher from Charlie Brown: "Whomp whomp whomp." Most times, I would just shake my head in compliance and do what was asked, regardless if I agreed with it or not it. I felt like it was better than having yet another argument.

Well, the dread of going home was growing to the point where I did not want to go home at all. I found comfort in being part of the crowd at the bar. I felt like I was wanted and what I had to say was important. Women laughed at my jokes and entertained my flirting.

With my wife, I didn't get any of this anymore. She was simply boring and equally demanding. I felt like at that point in our marriage, we were just going through the motions. We were married just because.

There was one day that changed that for me. My wife sent me a text to ask me to take her out later that day. I quickly responded, "Sure," while I was sitting there with my boys. When

I got home, I could feel that she suspected something but the way I was feeling, I ignored it.

She came in for a kiss. I immediately knew it was a trap. She was doing an undercover breathalyzer test. I quickly moved my head, so she wouldn't smell the beer on my breath. Why in the world did I do that?

Well, that did it for her. She started with her interrogation. "What took you so long? Was traffic really that bad that it took you forever to get home? Why didn't you text to say you would be late?" Then she asked the granddaddy of them all: "Have you been drinking?"

I rolled my eyes back and, in my mind, I thought, "Well Don, here is your chance to come clean. What are you going to do, bruh?" I took a deep breath before I belted out that I had been stopping off for Happy Hour with the fellas. I told her I was tired of coming home to arguments and eye-rolling by someone who I felt was more like a dictator than a wife.

I was honest and told her I needed to have a drink or two to delay coming home and to numb me from the arguments we often had when I walked through the door. Even though she was guilty of all the things I said, I had a gut feeling she would only focus on me stopping off before coming home. I didn't care though, I was relieved to finally get those things off my chest. It still hurts me to remember this period in our lives.

Telling her all of this was the only thing that seemed to make sense to me. Hell, I was caught, so I put it all out there. I wasn't sure if being honest with her would work at the time. I didn't know if she would judge me and totally ignore what I was saying to her or if she would hear my heart and attempt to sympathize.

I just knew I couldn't continue with Happy Hour therapy, because it was not good for me – nor would it be good for us. In the same breath, I didn't want to come home and feel like I had to walk on pins and needles just to keep the peace. I didn't want to negate my feelings any longer because I had an overbearing wife.

Whew, it was out there. I really didn't know or care how she was going to take it or receive it. All I knew was that I was glad that I got it off my chest and my truth was on the table. I was hoping that she would embrace me and that this would be an intimate moment.

Well, that didn't happen. After a few minutes of what seemed to silence and blank stares, I could feel that my wife was not ready to have a conversation about what I had just shared – or so I thought.

Instead of asking me what I felt or asking questions a loving wife would ask, like, "Honey, how can we overcome this?" or "Why didn't you say something sooner?" she led with "Are you an alcoholic?" Clearly, she hadn't taken the time to listen to a word I said, or she'd only heard what she wanted to hear. My enthusiasm quickly turned to regret.

I decided to take this opportunity to finally bare my soul to my wife. I told her that not only had I been chillin at the bar with the fellas, but that I had also entertained some foolish conversations and even flirted with other women since we had been married.

These conversations were very flattering and a switch from the normal household bill stuff. These women were giving me a breath of fresh air and I liked it – a lot. It was just what a brother needed and a break from the constant nagging that came with the territory of dealing with my wife.

Flirting with the ladies was a welcome distraction from my marriage issues. It was a respite from the heaviness of life. When I was single, flirting helped me deal with things in the past such as my poor relationship – and most times, nonexistent relationship – with my mother. I found myself flirting to cope with the problems in my marriage.

I thought laying it bear with my wife in that moment, that she would have empathy for me. She turned my confession around and accused me of not only making excuses for my bad choices but also for having the audacity to try to blame my poor choices on her. Little did she know, she was causing me more pain and agony by her response. She really had no idea that I dreaded going home to her.

All I wanted was to just finally be free to be upfront and honest with Ve. Instead, she put me in her version of Alcoholics Anonymous in that conversation. She just could not process how I was hurting and that this was my way of coping. This made me not want to go home even more.

I guess I never saw a problem with flirting because I never called or had contact with any of these women after the flirting. With these women, I never lied about being married or that I had a family. They didn't care and neither did I.

I simply looked at it as having a conversation with beautiful women who thought I was cute and funny. These conversations helped me escape real life. I didn't realize I had been using flirting as a coping mechanism until I went to my individual counseling sessions. My therapist helped me see this years later.

At one point, neither one of us attempted to accommodate each other's needs or even talk about them. We merely concentrated on relieving our stress in whatever capacity we could find: my wife engrossed herself in her degree and the kids, I watched hours of television, went to the gym, and hung out with the fellas basically every weekend.

There were even numerous times during this period when we were pretty sure we were headed to divorce court. One night, we even sat on the side of the bed, weighed our divorce options, and came up with a plan to cohabit until we could save enough money to go through with it. By the time our conversation was over, we came to the grim conclusion that we did not have the money to even submit the divorce paperwork.

We laughed so hard at how ridiculous this was, that we finally decided that we might as well stay together. We rationalized that we were great business partners and great parents, but we were not great as husband and wife. We told each other what awesome qualities the other had to make someone else happy.

The conversation then went from all the reasons why we should get a divorce to all the reasons why we should stay together, not as husband and wife but as roommates. It made perfect sense that we stay together for our kids.

Eventually, we grew to the point where we sought outside help for our own issues. My way to overcome the flirting and the Happy Hour therapy was by discussing my issues with my counselor.

I received coping tools I needed to help me find better ways to deal with my marital issues. I invested into a solid men's group at my church and began to share my thoughts and feelings with my wife.

Once my wife and I created a no-judgment zone and an open line of communication, I was able to tell my wife when I felt like I was struggling with flirting and needed her in an intimate way. Not only do I no longer stop off at the bar, but I can now have conversations with my wife instead of dreading going home.

Ask Yourself:

- Do you feel like the king of your castle or just some dude who pays the bills? Why or why not?
- Is your house a home? Why/why not?
- Have you ever felt like you just did not want to go home?
- If you did, how did you handle it?
- If you have issues at home, what have you done to correct them?
- Do you have an area in your home where you can collect your thoughts, like a man cave?
- Is there a woman or are there women you need to cut lose that are causing you to not honor your wife?
- What is one thing you can do to cut those ties?

Instant Replay: Notes to myself

6 Nah, I'm Good
"A problem is a chance for you to do your best." Duke Ellington

"Nah, I'm good." Three words most men like to use when we don't want to talk. I wonder how many times you have used them. For years, this was my motto because I just didn't want to talk about issues with my wife. Hell, there were times I didn't even want to talk to my wife. She had a Ph.D. in Work-a-Brother's Nerves.

As men, it is easier for us to say, "I'm good" when we are pissed off or upset. But very rarely will a woman hear us say that our feelings are hurt. If you are anything like how I was, you probably feel that you must portray an "I am tougher than leather" persona, regardless of how hurt you may really be. I get it, brother. I was there for most of my life.

My truth is that I was deeply hurt by the plethora of arguments with my wife. If I am going to be totally honest with you, I have to say, I really disliked my wife in those moments and sometimes days after an exchange. I didn't like the way she made me feel. Before you say it, I know I am responsible for my own feelings and emotions. I also know that I shouldn't give anyone control over my emotions.

But brotha, this was my wife. I was shocked that this amazing woman, who had pledged her unconditional love to me, had turned out to be someone who would hurt me repeatedly; for years. In my mind, my wife was not supposed to hurt me. I did not say, "I do" to being hurt by the woman I loved.

Initially, I would argue back and say hurtful things to my wife just to get her to leave me the hell alone. This was my MO for years too. I am not proud of this. I also must put this out there: I cussed my wife out a lot. I called her out of her name several times, more than I care to remember. I have even threatened to divorce her numerous times.

This was my destructive behavior for years. I took this stance with anybody that hurt me. This included my mother, my family members, or anyone else who I felt crossed me, betrayed my trust, and yes, hurt me emotionally.

When I used to get together with the fellas, we would all be sitting around drinking and complaining about our wives. To an extent, we all had some of the same issues but none of us would jump out there and lay it on the line to say we were hurting. Not one!

We looked forward to getting together as a way of escaping home life and our wives. We partied hard and then dreaded going back home. None of us ended the weekend feeling any better than when we started it. Looking back on it, I can't believe we did this for years.

Another way I would express myself to avoid sharing my feelings was through the silent treatment. Yes, I know this is a very childish. However, it was an effective method when my wife wouldn't leave me alone or accept my "I'm good." The silent treatment was easy to do, and I liked it.

Our joke is that she used to be an incessant Chihuahua who would follow me from room to room to get in the last word. Picture us running around the house yelling at each other. I would have to explode into a tirade of cuss words to get her to stand down. This chick was vicious.

Because of this, I would dig deep when I felt like she had my back up against a wall and that she would not let something go. I would go days without speaking to my wife because that was my way of getting back at her.

Hell, I withheld sex too. I knew it drove her crazy. Ha, I enjoyed getting under her skin. We had a twisted marriage back then. Whew, I thank God for therapy and a whole lot of patience.

In reality, problems do not solve themselves through the silent treatment. Every single relationship needs communication. Countries go to war over stalled talks, players hold out from practice because of stalled contract negotiations, and marriages fail due to a lack of effective communication.

Even though I thought I had the upper, I was not helping the situation one bit. I only added to and escalated the confusion. I allowed myself to be disconnected in my marriage. I unplugged from my wife when I should have been dialed in. I, figuratively, walked away from my wife when I should have stayed in the game and been a team player. Nothing ever got resolved because I refused to sit at the table and have a discussion with my wife.

I know dudes who would die a thousand deaths before they would ever admit to anyone that what their wife said or did hurt them to their core. I know, because I was that dude. Admitting I was hurt by my wife seemed like I would be suggesting that I was lacking in the manhood department.

This was then multiplied with the other disappointments and rejections I felt in life. I had conveniently tucked these away with the all betrayals I have experienced in my life too.

Seriously, one day, I looked up and my life looked like that "new math" they are teaching the kids in schools today. I just couldn't figure out what the hell happened or how I got here.

Side note, if you are a dad, you know exactly what I am talking about. You feel like you need a master's degree in Quantum Rocket Science to simply teach your middle-schooler algebra.

If we are going to be real about it, we tend to judge our wives or our girlfriends from those past hurts and rejections. Even though we will not admit it to them or anyone else for that matter, some of us are still living in that place.

This is not fair to your wife or fiancé. Living like this is very unhealthy when you are attempting to create a good relationship with the women we love.

I've heard men and women alike say that they will never allow themselves to be hurt again. Most times they are referring to giving someone their love, trust, and even the big one, their heart. Trying to protect ourselves from being hurt is counterproductive and typically results in all parties involved getting hurt in the long run.

At the beginning of my marriage, I quickly learned that at the times I needed my wife the most, she would not allow me to be vulnerable with her. For some reason, it was like she had a mental block to allowing me to really be me. She would tell me to "get over it," whatever my "it" was in that moment. I hated her for it since her response was so crushing.

The very person I wanted to talk to would repeatedly shut me up and shut me down. This propelled me to use "I'm good" whenever she did get around to asking me what was wrong whenever I had an attitude. I just couldn't take the chance of her dismissing me and hurting my feelings again.

The road to being able to finally talk to my wife about my true feelings took years. Initially, when I stopped hiding behind "I'm good" and I started expressing myself to her, she was not ready to hear me.

One day, as I was trying to tell her how I felt, she just would not be quiet. I yelled at the top of my lungs, "Shut the f**k up and let me talk!"

It jarred her and I could tell she was in her feelings. This woman had the audacity to stand there, with an indignant look on her face and with her arms crossed because she couldn't believe that I just went off on her. Really?

I then asked her, as calmly as I could, to simply be quiet and listen to me for a moment. I asked her to not try to fix me in that moment, but to let me get my thoughts and feelings out. I even warned her that if she didn't give me the safe space to do it, there were plenty of women who would eagerly listen to me.

Man, her face was scrunched up then, and I really could not tell if she was going to listen to me or not. I threw a "Hail Mary" and let it all out. That is when I became liberated and free.

The truthful yet painful conversations that stemmed from that initial conversation with my wife were eye-opening. Some were so heated that we wouldn't speak to each other for days. Other conversations drew us closer together. During some of those discussions, she and I both worked extremely hard to listen to each other without judgment. It was no easy feat.

This was not an overnight sensation. This took time and a lot of hits and misses. These moments eventually strengthened my communication skills to the point where I finally felt free to tell her when something she said to me was hurtful or when I didn't appreciate something she said to me.

When I decided to no longer hide behind "I'm good," I discovered the power of sharing my feelings and thoughts without the fear of being shut down. Seeking therapy helped with this as well. Through therapy, we learned how to establish boundaries in our marriage. We each learned to say what we had to say with love.

Once we began to do this, we were able to respect each other more and we grew closer by using effective communication tools and skills. "I'm good" slowly left my vocabulary for good.

Ask Yourself:

- Can you tell your wife or significant other if what she has said to you is hurtful or has hurt your feelings?
- Do you revert to the *Silent Treatment?* If so, what has it gotten you?
- Do you feel like you have a voice when you have a dispute with your lady/wife?
- Have you ever shut down during a disagreement or an argument? How do you rebound?
- Do you keep a mental note of the things your lady/wife says that could be hurtful?
- When are you going to let those things go so you can grow and move forward?

Instant Replay: Notes to myself

7 Finally, Owning My Sh*t

"Wanna fly, you got to give up the shit that weighs you down."
Toni Morrison

It was a Thanksgiving afternoon that I will never, ever forget. Thanksgiving is one of my favorite holidays and for obvious reasons, a brother loves to eat.

That afternoon, I did what I normally did every Thanksgiving Day, I checked the computer for game times and to see who my Dallas Cowboys would beat up on that Turkey Day. I was also looking forward to spending this day with my wife, my kids, and my in-laws, who were spending the holiday with us.

Upon checking the stats on the computer, I noticed my wife's Facebook account was open on another tab. This was not unusual because no one used this computer but her, and on rare occasions, me. I immediately thought, "Let me check my Facebook page, really quick."

I was going to stir the pot for the upcoming game and to remind all my Washington Redskins friends that their team, as usual, was going to be basement dwellers and why they don't get Thanksgiving Day games.

I clicked on the tab where my wife's page was open to log her off and to log into my account. I noticed her Facebook page was open to her message inbox and the last note she had read was open. It was a long message from some dude she went to high school with. From what I read in those five minutes, he was clearly gassing her head up. He dropped all the "game", so he could get next to my wife.

He didn't know me, so of course he had no problem disrespecting me. As much as I wanted to log off, I could not take my eyes off the screen. I know first-hand that dudes can be sneaky. I started reading some of her responses.

Even though she did not blatantly agree with his words, it felt like she had encouraged this behavior. Even though she responded that she was married, she never told him to stop messaging her.

I took a deep breath and paused, because in this case, there was nothing she could have said to get out of this one. She had been caught. I was beyond angry. I was seeing red. I was upside down mad. I needed Jesus to take the wheel at that very moment.

My in-laws were downstairs excitedly preparing for our family dinner and I was upstairs deciding how I was going to make it through the day. I decided I was going to go to my sister's house to get a break from my wife and this revelation.

I grabbed a duffel bag out the closet and started putting some clothes in it. There was no way I was going to stay here in this house with her. There was no way I was going to fake the funk just because her folks were downstairs.

I shot her a text to ask her to come upstairs. I could not wait to show her what I found. I was seething. When she came upstairs, I simply said to her, "Ve, what is this shit in your Facebook inbox?" Believe it or not, this was the first time in a long time that I did not call her out of her name, even though the thought crossed my mind.

I let my wife know straight up that I wasn't snooping when I came across her inbox. We had never had a reason to check each other's accounts or phones leading up to this day. I calmly told Ve that I was jumping on my Facebook page to harass my boys about the upcoming games.

I was trying my best to contain myself because my children and my in-laws were moving around in the house. Because of this, I hissed through clenched teeth, "I'm out."

My wife immediately went into panic mode. She gently pleaded with me for me not to leave. She tried to explain what I had seen, but I was not trying to hear none of it. I felt I was double-crossed, hoodwinked, and violated. I just wanted to go.

All I could think about at that moment were all the sacrifices I made for her and my children. This included working two jobs, so she could stay home to run her home daycare, complete her bachelor's degree, and homeschool our children. What kind of woman does that to a man who is taking care of the home? Apparently, my wife.

She asked me once again to let her explain. For some odd reason, I told her I would listen to what she had to say for five minutes. I'm not sure how or why, but I stopped packing and just sat on the bed. She began to tell me how lonely she felt and how I didn't look at her or treat her the way I used to.

I wanted to yell at her, *"Woman, what do you mean, you're lonely? When I'm home with you, there is always drama. Other times, I'm so tired that everything is a blur. I need to be a father to these kids and truth be told, your sweatpants and mixed-matched socks ain't doing it for me!"* But I kept my cool and chose to listen to her.

She told me how this guy made her feel like she was important and how he validated her. She said he complimented her on all the stuff he saw her doing on Facebook. She shared how it all started off with small compliments. She said initially she didn't see anything wrong with him messaging her, since she had other guy friends from high school doing the same thing.

She even reminded me that some of them I was cool with. I thought, "Wow, this dude was really trying to put in work to get my woman. I guess he didn't know she comes with bills, a car note, and a mouth for days."

She told me to look at the last few messages again. She said that had I read all the way to the very last messages, I would have seen how she told him his recent comments were out of bounds. Honestly, I only saw the inappropriate stuff he wrote. I told her I didn't need to see the messages again.

She pleaded with me to please stay at least through Thanksgiving dinner. Her parents were downstairs with the kids. She didn't want to disrupt Thanksgiving, even though those messages had already done that for me.

I asked her to leave the room because I needed to collect my thoughts. Really, I just wanted her out of my face before I said something really crazy to her. I walked into our bathroom and looked at myself in the mirror. I had a decision to make.

I was so torn. Usually it's the man standing on the other side of this conversation asking for forgiveness for some indiscretion. So, this was not only awkward, but it was also unfamiliar territory for me. I began to think about my children and how much I would miss seeing them every day. How I would miss tucking them into bed every night.

In my opinion, children need both parents in their lives. I grew up in a single parent home and I would be lying if I said I didn't wish I could have come home to find both parents waiting to see how my school day was, or even take family trips together.

I thought about all the failed marriages on my side of the family. My grandparents were divorced, my parents were divorced, and now, would my name be added to the ledger? I paced between my bathroom and bedroom for what seemed to be hours. I was thinking long and hard about what my wife had shared. I was so pissed I could see sideways. I wondered why she would choose to entertain this guy.

I felt for a split second that my manhood had been challenged. This dude was rapping to my wife. I thought to myself, "I'm a good dude. I'm a provider. I bring my check home every time I get paid. What happened? How could she do this to ME?" I was mad that I couldn't even answer my own questions.

So, I decided to do something that I had not done in a while. I took this to God in prayer. I remembered my grandmother's words from when I was a kid: "Son, when you don't know what to do, just pray." That is exactly what I did. I prayed like I was back in Sunday school.

You know how people say some things are like riding a bike? That you never forget how to do it? Well, I think that applies to prayer because after a few minutes, I prayed like I was T.D. Jakes at a revival service.

After replaying the last few years of my marriage in my mind and then the conversation I'd had with my wife a few minutes prior, the moment of truth arrived. I opened the bedroom door and walked downstairs to be with my family.

I quietly told my wife that I needed time to process what she had said. I told her I would stay in the house long enough to figure out what my next move was going to be. I just did not have it in me to stay in this house with her.

In those days following what I perceived to be the ultimate betrayal, my emotions were all over the map. My thoughts ranged from "F**k this b***h, I am not trying to hear a word she has to say," to me trying to figure out how was I going to get past this, or "Do I just tuck this situation away and move forward?"

To top it all off, I had feelings of helplessness. All the negative feelings of past hurts and pains, along with the strong feelings of rejection, all seemed to surface at once. I felt myself slowly slipping into victim mode. This was a deep dark place for me. I felt like I was drowning at times.

Sometimes, I just wanted to be left alone. I felt my actions were warranted because my wife had deeply hurt me. This was a place where I could have a pity party and make up reasons why I no longer needed her or anyone else in my life who crossed me.

I wanted so bad to leave her. Where I was torn, though, was that she was the mother of my children and my wife, the one who I'd promised to love no matter what — all the days of my life. I questioned whether this made me a liar if I turned and walked away and then I wondered if I would still be considered a man if I stayed.

There had been times in my life where I had cut off my nose to spite my face. I wanted to do it again. But in this case, the stakes were that much higher. My children would be directly affected by my choice.

So many times, I wished I could have had a conversation with some of my closest friends, but to be honest, I was too embarrassed to pick up the phone and bare my truth. I feared what they would have said or even thought – about her and about me.

I simply was at a crossroad. I felt my manhood was on the line and that I had to do something, anything. Like at the beginning of a football game, I wanted to do a coin toss – Heads, I stay, Tails, I go. If only it was that easy.

Eventually, I got tired of this tug-of-war within myself. I finally asked myself, "Don, what did you do to contribute to this entire fiasco?" I realized that I had to take responsibility for my part in my wife's year-long emotional affair.

I know what you are wondering: "Seriously, bruh, you really gonna let her off the hook? How are you at fault for her actions? That was foul and mad disrespectful."

Believe it or not, I was responsible because I had stopped being a husband to my wife. I was so drained from all of our previous arguments and so caught up with work, I stopped paying attention to her.

This opened the door for someone else to come in and do my job, make my wife feel like a queen. I really thought that because I financially took care of everything she wanted or needed, that I was doing my job.

I used to tell my wife, during those ugly arguments, that she should find someone to make her happy since she made me feel like I was not a good husband. That old saying: "You best be careful what you ask for, because you just might get it."

Well, yeah, that's what happened to us. My wife got what I had spoken in heated conversations – a guy who made her happy. She loved the conversations and how he made her feel. She had even shared how she started looking forward to meeting him on the chat. They were the highlight of her days.

My wife tried to communicate her feelings to me. She wanted to let me know what she needed but because I was absorbed in providing, I just did not hear her. This is why I say communication is key every day in every relationship, especially in marriage.

My wife's need for validation should have been met by God first and then by me, but it simply wasn't. She eventually realized she had shut God out of this area of her life because she was focused on what she didn't receive from me: attention, affection, and love. We had become estranged, even though we slept in the same bed every night.

I rode an internal emotional roller coaster and it seemed like that ride was never going to end. I fought thoughts in my head for weeks that said, "Ask her how she could do that to you? Hold this over her head. Point the finger at her and blame her for hurting you." I realized that deciding to point the finger at her meant three more would be pointing back to me.

These thoughts were all counterproductive, although they seemed like they were normal, and for the most part, justified my wanting to be done with her. Those thoughts would do nothing to promote healing and growth in my marriage. I did the most mature thing I have ever done in my life: I chose to forgive her.

After all, she didn't get to that place of feeling lonely and needing validation all by herself. I searched long and hard and wondered where I needed to improve and to simply do better as a husband. This is a question most people never think to ask themselves in a situation like this, especially if they feel they were the one done wrong.

Facts: even after praying, forgiving her, and taking full responsibility for my role in my wife's emotional affair and my actions that led up to that situation, even though I had forgiven her in my heart, I still felt like I was in a weird space. Yes, I had forgiven her. However, I struggled with, "How do I forgive myself?"

I knew that part of this was a direct result of my behavior over the years, along with not being emotionally and mentally present in my marriage. I attempted to forgive me and my shortcomings.

Looking back on the chain of events, I still can't believe I took the high road in this matter. Had this happened earlier in my marriage, there would have been no us, and no book.

In trying to give myself grace for the role I played, I began to see my wife and her situation through the eyes of compassion. I didn't see her anymore as a woman who was trying to cheat on me, but as a woman who was broken and needed me – her husband – to pick her up, to restore her, and to love her unconditionally.

I'm not going to lie and say that we rode into the sunset in love overnight. It took time and effort on both our parts. I remember one day thinking about how much I loved my wife and kids. I really did not want to divorce this woman. I prayed more than I ever had in my life combined. I know my wife prayed too. I asked God to give me the strength to make it through this. With His help, I knew that this too shall pass.

One morning, while my wife was asleep, I just lay there and looked at her. I felt a new level of love for her that I can't explain. I knew deep down in my heart that we were going to be alright. I rolled over, kissed my wife, and I whispered in her ear that I loved her and forgave her.

Not long after that day, we decided to seek therapy to work out our own individual issues. I promised Ve that I would never bring up the emotional affair up again. That was the first time in my life, I decided to forgive and to love someone unconditionally who had hurt me.

Ask Yourself:

- Are you a grudge-holder?
- Do you forgive easily? Why or why not?
- Can you forgive your lady/wife and not hold that issue against her?
- Have you ever listened without the intent to judge what is being said?
- Do you take responsibility for your actions even when you are wronged?
- Are you able to show empathy when you are the one hurting?
- Could you stay in your relationship even though society says you have a legitimate right to "roll out"?

Instant Replay: Notes to myself

8 Counseling - Who Needs That?

"If you can't be advised you can't advance." Bernard Kelvin Clive

Back in the day, when my wife would talk to me about counseling, I would tell her flat out that I did not need it. I believed that it was a complete waste of time and there was nothing wrong with me. My response to her was always, "I'm good". After all, my wife and I tried marriage counseling, not at just one, but several churches.

It seemed like we argued with each other more after those church counseling sessions, so we decided not to go anymore. My wife's pushing me to go to counseling fell on deaf ears for years after that. I was thinking if it is so good and beneficial then you need to go.

My perception of individual counseling, at that time in my life, was that it was for people who couldn't get their lives together. I really believed it was for people who had serious problems. As far as I was concerned, I was fine. I went to work every day.

I was an active participant with my children and their activities. I had a close network of friends who I had great relationships with and who were always there for me when I needed to talk. Clearly, I was not a person who needed counseling.

Besides, no one I knew had sought therapy to deal with their problems or issues. I often thought, "How would people look at me if they found out I went to counseling? I am not falling apart mentally or socially.

Yes, I had marital issues like everyone else, but we weren't physically assaulting each other." I couldn't understand how going to counseling would help or fix the problems with my wife or in my marriage. I simply thought we had the same problems my friends and their wives had.

Even though in the back of my mind, I felt this was not normal to be arguing with my wife all the time, it did seem normal since we knew other couples who were doing the exact same thing.

In my opinion, they seemed to work their way through their issues or they were doing one hell of a great job of faking it like I had been doing. To me, things seemed to end up working themselves out at some point or their marriages simply ended in divorce.

I remember my wife approaching me yet again about the subject of me going to counseling. As usual I wasn't trying to hear her. This time was different. I gave her a chance. I listened with the intent of hearing what she was saying to me.

My wife has a way of oozing whatever she is saying with milk and honey. This time was no different. But it was, I wanted to hear her out. I used to barely listen when my wife would talk to me. I ask you, what man hasn't at some point in their marriage?

As she ran down her list of reasons why I needed to go to counseling, I was almost offended with what she was saying. It felt like she was pointing out everything that was wrong with me. She made me feel like I was the reason we are having all these issues.

In the past, this would have been my excuse to shut the conversation down and to walk out of the room. I must say I am extremely proud of myself. Like a wide receiver with a strong safety bearing down on him in the center of the field, I stayed with the route, made the catch and took the big hit. I still held onto the ball for the first down.

After what seemed like a five-hour doctoral dissertation, I reluctantly agreed to see a therapist. This agreement carried with it some strong stipulations. These stipulations were to discourage my wife from following through with making me see a counselor.

Stipulation number one was that I had to have a male therapist because I didn't want to see a woman. In my mind, I already knew she would side with my wife in these discussions. Unbeknownst to me, a therapist is neutral. Stipulation number two was that the sessions had to fit within my schedule and be in our local area.

I refused to drive more than ten minutes to sit on someone's couch. Stipulation three was that she had to do all the legwork. She was tasked with finding the therapist, making my initial appointment and making sure our insurance covered the sessions.

I thought this was a fair trade off since she was the one who insisted that I go to counseling. I really thought she would drop the ball and all this counseling talk would just fall to the wayside.

Not only did this woman agree to do all of this, with a smirk on her face I might add, to my surprise, she had all of it completed within two days. She had an appointment for me in the same week, damn! My wife is a true champion! So, guess who was going to counseling?

Two days later, the day arrived. It was time to attend my first official session of couch time. I pulled up in the parking lot. I must have sat in the car for what seemed to be an eternity. I took a deep breath and whispered to myself, "Don, it's game time".

I went into the office and filled out some paperwork. I anxiously waited to get in the game or in this case, hit the couch. I had no clue what to expect. I was nervous, but I wanted to be able to show my wife that I did it.

The counselor was cool and from his approach, I could tell he could see my reluctance to open up and talk. He began by slowly working his way into why I was there and into my personal life. I answered a lot of questions and was trying to read this brother, while I'm sure he was reading me.

Forty-five minutes into the hour session I finally started to open up about my life. Initially, I was all over the map from my childhood to the present, to college and then back to my childhood and even my marriage. All of sudden, my session was over.

I was upset about it. I felt like yelling, "NO! Wait! I am just getting started". He reassured me that I did well for my first session and that he would see me next week. I booked that appointment before I left.

The day of my second session arrived and I was looking forward to it. During that session, we immediately got right to it. This time we focused a little more on specific issues. I was letting it all hang out. I was telling and sharing everything. I did so without fear of judgment or what he would think of me.

I felt free to be honest and open. I felt no fear. I enjoyed the fact he allowed me to talk without interrupting me. During the session, he offered me better ways to look at situations and to resolve conflict.

I continued to see him for months. I'm not going to lie to you, there were times when I was in counseling, bawling like a baby. It was exactly what I needed to begin healing from my past. It also felt great to be that free and not have someone look at me like I was crazy.

My therapist was fully invested in me improving myself and my life. He even offered to see my wife in one of my sessions. Initially, I didn't want to, but I knew I needed to if I was going to continue in my journey to becoming a whole man.

That was a turning point in our marriage. She cried. I cried. We left that session with handouts and worksheets about effective communication. We left with tools to become better towards each other.

Whenever we felt arguments start to rise up, we would reference those sheets. We also gave each other permission to walk away from an argument if it got too heated. This gave space and time think rationally. We gave each other permission to come back later when the tensions simmered.

We even discovered that if we hugged or kissed the other person when tensions were flaring, this de-escalated the arguments very quickly. We would say to each other, "You look real crazy trying to argue with someone who is trying to kiss or hug you."

I now work to make a conscious effort to not read something into a situation that is not there nor, do I allow myself to be dragged into unhealthy, unproductive conversations with people that will do nothing but stress me out.

Therapy also helped me stopped flirting. I take full ownership for my own actions. I can clearly see the role I played in a lot of the foolish conversations with women and the many senseless, needless arguments that I have had with my wife over the years.

The counseling helped me first and foremost, identify areas in my life and my thought process that were just for a lack of better words - off. It's different when someone you don't know personally tells you that what you are saying, or thinking is just another way or excuse to stay guarded or to shift blame to someone else.

I quickly learned that some our friends are not even going to tell us the real truth like a counselor would because, real talk, some of them are dealing with similar issues. They will co-sign some of the crazy stuff you say out your mouth about your wife, your life and things in general. Some will even allow us to do wrong instead of encouraging us to make the right choices for our lives.

My therapist was not playing those games with me. He helped

me realize that my wife nor anyone else in my past that had hurt me was not my mother. I could no longer hold my wife accountable for the things in my past. I could not hold her accountable for stuff in our past.

I had to acknowledge that those things were in the past and that I could not move forward or become productive by living from a place of past hurts or frustrations. I understand that my past and my present could no longer share the same space. I also had to accept that I could not control the family I was born into. I also did not have to subscribe to the things that people say run in the family.

I have something I want to share with you. No one knows this unless they read it right here. I was diagnosed with depression. Whew! I can't believe I just shared that. I had no idea that was one of the reasons I was self-sabotaging and so angry all the time.

I was hurting, and I hated where my life had been. I was depressed that I had been at odds with my wife for years that money wasn't the way I felt it should have been and just overall overwhelm with my life. It was hard to hear but I was relieved to know why I had mood swings. This diagnosis was a turning point for me.

So dear brother, if you are on the fence about going to

counseling, let me push you of that fence and onto a therapist's couch. We need you to be whole. I found counseling to be rewarding and liberating. I am clear that there is no shame in taking positive steps to improve myself and my marriage.

I challenge you to stop hiding behind thinking you're good and that counseling is only for people with issues. You very well may be dealing with depression, PTSD or any other issues that are preventing you from living your best life. Let today be the last day you walk this alone.

I truly believe that counseling is one of those best kept secrets, because now I enjoy going and I look forward to dumping all my issues on that couch, so I can go home a little freer, a little lighter. I also receive information to not just to improve myself but to improve my marriage and the way I relate with people in general.

In short, my wife is not my enemy and I will not judge her or look at her from any place other than a place of love and respect. Is my wife perfect? Nope! But neither am I. Counseling and tons of prayer have helped me turn my marriage and life around. I constantly think, "Wow", my wife was right. I'm so glad I made time for counseling. I no longer make excuses for my behavior or blame others. It was the best decision I have ever made.

Ask Yourself:

- Do you have reservations about counseling? Why or why not?
- Have you ever sought out therapy for yourself?
- Are you afraid to discuss past hurts or pain? Why or why not?
- When was the last time you were open and honest about your feelings without feeling less than a man?
- Are you willing to take positive steps to change your unhealthy behaviors no matter what they are?
- Can you handle the truth without "kirking out"?
- If not, what is one way you can react positively next time you have conflict?

Instant Replay: Notes to myself

9 Don't Call It A Comeback

"You can't go back and make a new start, but you can start right now and make a brand-new ending." James R. Sherman

A few years after I started therapy, I got a girlfriend. You read that right, maaaaaaaan, I got a girlfriend. She came into my life at the perfect time. She was everything I needed at that point in my life.

I needed her, and she needed me. She was there for me at my weak moments. I could not wait to see her at the end of a long day. Some days, she was all I could think about. I still go to my cell phone during my work day to text her. My girlfriend listens to me. She loves me. She allows me to be vulnerable. She gives me a shoulder to cry on. She is perfect for me.

Before you slam this book closed and request a refund, you can chill because my girlfriend is my wife. When my life changed, she changed. When I was able to communicate more effectively, she was able to receive what I was saying.

She no longer judged me and I was no longer this angry guy. Our relationship grew to a whole other level. We were no longer just husband and wife. We finally became lovers and friends.

I shared some crazy things we experienced in our marriage. Some of those things would crush other marriages. But at the end of the day, we still loved each other. I believe those things we overcame made us grow closer together. I heard Pastor Joel Osteen say, "Your mess can become your message".

I know for a fact that the problems Ve and I overcame, became our message. We can help couples work through marital issues and the challenges of trying to communicate so their spouses can hear them.

Many people have asked me, "How did you and Vedia do it? How did you guys manage to stay together through her issues and through all of yours? How did you forgive her emotional affair?" I am not going to deceive you and say that it was easy.

We had to be willing to take the necessary steps to improve ourselves, so we could have the mental space to come together and work on us. The process was not without some bumps in the road and a few setbacks.

Yet, we were determined. We knew that we could be successful as Don and Tanya, the husband and wife team, through counseling, prayer and of course, time. This is where the shift happened.

I started doing things to bring the romance back to our relationship. When we were dating, I used to bring my wife flowers. I decided to start that up again. I started stopping at the store to get her flowers on Fridays. Joe, the flower guy at the store, would somehow remember what flowers I bought the week before and would kindly remind me.

He also knew my wife because she shopped in that store, so he had an idea of what she liked. They would have casual conversations, so he put a lot of effort into helping me pick the perfect flowers for her. He would even do special floral arrangements and wouldn't charge me extra. That dude had a green thumb for real.

Another one of my favorite things I did for my wife was to draw her nice bubble baths. We have one of those big tubs in our bathroom that can fit two people. I would fill the tube full of hot water and some good smelling bubble bath solution. I make sure to pour her a glass of wine and to light her favorite candles.

You also know your boy had her favorite old school slow jams playing, which always included one of our favorite groups, Jodeci. I would let her lay it that water for good 30 to 40 minutes or so just to unwind. I even would refill it with more hot water if it got too cool.

Then came my favorite part, I would join her. We would laugh, or we would be silent. We would sometimes talk other times we would cry. It was a safe space just to be free and bare our souls to each other.

On some evenings, we try to walk together after I get off work to reconnect and to talk without interruptions from our kids, who are now young adults and teenagers.

I also decided to step my game up by taking my wife out on dates. For years, I usually went out with the fellas, while she was home with the kids. Now, I look forward to seeing my wife put on something sexy and her smell good stuff, just for me.

Going out with Ve, helped us to get back to having fun in our marriage. Our sex life was no longer boring or routine and it no longer felt like another thing to begrudgingly check off of my "to-do list."

She became my best friend and my girlfriend. We would go to jazz clubs in DC or wherever there was a live band. We both love music so we looked for events, so we could literally dance the night away. We would laugh and have fun like two grown kids. The woman who I fell in love with and who I gave my heart to back in 1999 was new and improved.

I am so happy I chose to see it through not only with myself but with my wife. We realized there were no big I's nor little U's nor one offense greater than the other. We both made our fair share of mistakes in our nineteen years of marriage.

We both have taken responsibility for our marriage being very dysfunctional. Thank God, we were and still are committed to going forward victoriously, together. Attending therapy sessions, being transparent with my wife and simply communicating my needs were the best things I could have ever done for me.

This shift and willingness to change for the better opened doors neither of us could have ever imagined. We went from fighting with each other to fighting for our marriage. We now share our story of love, hope and forgiveness nationally.

We've been featured in ESSENCE.com for their Valentine's Day Black Love Feature. Our comeback has been shared on panels at the Congressional Black Caucus, NAACP, as well as on The Tom Joyner Morning Show, Huffington Post and countless interviews on local DC television and radio.

Imagine our surprise when we were contacted about sharing our story on "THE" Oprah Winfrey Network to be featured on the hot show, Black Love DOC.

Even with all of this going on, trust me, we are not perfect by any stretch of the imagination. We still have moments when things get a little heated, however, we now have the tools to diffuse it quickly. We are purposefully making conscious choices to be more understanding and forgiving to each other.

We realize we both are a work in progress and that our marriage takes effort to be successful. My manhood was on the line and I was on a slippery slope. I went from flirting with poor choices to being committed to myself, my wife and my kids. As a man, I am very proud to say we are on the come up, so picture us rollin'.

Ask Yourself:

- When was the last time **YOU** planned a romantic outing with your lady/wife?
- Do you see your lady/wife as your lover and friend? If NO, why? If YES, why?
- Do you genuinely enjoy your lady's/wife's company?
- What can you do **TODAY** to rekindle the romance in your relationship?

Instant Replay: Notes to myself

THE GAME PLAN

"Change will not come if we wait for some other person or some other time. We are the ones we've been waiting for. We are the change that we seek."

—President Barack Obama

I want you to use this area to map out a game plan for positive change in your life. Think about small things you can do today. Consider having a heart to heart with yourself today.

How have you compromised your manhood? Have you entertained foolish conversations? Have you even involved yourself with another woman? Can you look on the back of your insurance card and call for the mental wellness number? Are you able to stop off and buy fresh flowers?

Mother, Thank You for Leaving

One thing that worked for me for my healing was to write my mother a letter. Now, keep in mind, she has never seen or read this letter. She doesn't even know it exists. Yet, writing this letter was therapeutic for me. It helped me get my feelings out on paper for my mother. It is below:

****

I am not sure what makes a person just walk away and basically have nothing to do with the upbringing of their child. I could understand if you were trying to venture out to make a better life for you and your children. In this equation, it seems like the better life you sought was just for you, solely. Did you even care about me or even what happened to me? Or did you just assume my dad and my grandmother had it? Guess what? They did and they did a wonderful job raising yours truly.

My grandmother gave me more love then I could ever imagine. She took me to church. She and my dad taught me right from wrong. She was there for all my bumps and bruises. My dad did the best he could with what he knew to provide for and to take care of his only son. Although they left this earth far too soon, they gave me the tools to get started in life without you. I remember at my dad's funeral, you offered me absolutely nothing. But then again, I expected nothing from you.

I will admit that life for me was no crystal staircase. I had to grow up fast and I had to figure things out for myself. In your absence, I made a choice to live and not die when many people and family members thought I would be a victim of my circumstances.

In your absence, I did more than just survive, I thrived. I am a college graduate and honorably served my country. The icing on the cake is that I have a wife of nineteen years, three wonderful children who I love more then they will ever know.

There were some tough times and I had to work two jobs to make ends meet. I thank you for leaving and being selfish 'cause if you stayed in my life there is a good chance I wouldn't be the man I am today. I can't believe I let your absence affect me for years instead of seeing it as a blessing.

Because you decided to leave and not be a mother, I developed a strong sense of determination and purpose. I am now capable of doing anything with nothing. So yeah mom, thanks for leaving!

If there is someone you need to write, whether you share the letter with them or not, use mine as a template. It is written exactly how I wrote it. Do the same. Our manhood is daily on the line. This is a step to reclaim it.

About the Author

Donald F Barnett III is a Marriage Advocate, Black Male Relationship Expert and Empowerment Speaker. Don uses comedy and his real-life experiences to speak this truth about marriage, parenting, family and being a Black Man in the 21st century.

He is a lifetime member of Omega Psi Phi Fraternity Incorporated. Don is affectionately known in his community as Coach Don to the kids he has coached in soccer and football. He mentors middle school boys in the life skills they will need as well as exposes them to cultural and fun activities.

He has been featured in Black Love DOC on OWNTV, Essence Magazine, and Congressional Black Caucus.

Don is a husband, father and new grandfather.

Social media IG/TW: @DonBarnettIII.

Made in the USA
San Bernardino, CA
22 October 2018